T0078070

Like the Sun In the Skies, We Rise!

Karla Davis Mason

BALBOA.PRESS

A DIVISION OF HAY HOUSE

Balboa Press books may be ordered through booksellers or by contacting:

Balboa Press
A Division of Hay House
1663 Liberty Drive
Bloomington, IN 47403
www.balboapress.com
844-682-1282

Scripture quotations marked NLT are taken from the Holy Bible, New Living Translation, copyright © 1996, 2004, 2007. Used by permission of Tyndale House Publishers, Inc. Carol Stream, Illinois 60188. All rights reserved. Website

Print information available on the last page.

ISBN: 978-1-9822-5678-4 (sc)
ISBN: 978-1-9822-5677-7 (hc)
ISBN: 978-1-9822-5676-0 (e)

Library of Congress Control Number: 2020920257

Balboa Press rev. date: 07/07/2023

Written expressions created to inspire thought,
reflection, understanding, hope & healing.

Through the Vicissitudes of Life, We Can Rise!

Contents

Preface ix

Fear Not My Skin, Look Deep Within! 3
Who Taught You To Hate? 7
Dear Pop 11
Still I Heal 15
Sincerely, Melanated Queens 19
Escape.From.Sunken.Places. 23
What Would They Do If They Really Knew? 27
Yet I Rise 29
He Wept 31
True to You 33
Just The Way I Am 35
Reflections, Reflections, Reflections 39
Worthy 43
Dreams.Detours.Destinations. 47
Revered Yet Feared 51
The Thin Line 53
Black Enough 57
From Darkness to Light 61
Crown & Glory Within 63
Luvin' My Authenticity 65
Magnificent Melanation 67
What's It Like, My Father? 71

Reflections 73
Acknowledgements 74

Preface

When I was very young, I didn't always know how to verbally express all the things I was feeling inside. Poetry became a wonderful, therapeutic outlet for me...and it's one I still use today. Poetry is an individual sport of sorts that no one else can really critically challenge.

Through poetry we have the freedom to be as direct or abstract, as raw or eloquent as we want to be. Our words don't have to be grammatically correct, specific, or make perfect sense to anyone but us. We can express ourselves, reach others and bring awareness to things some might otherwise find uncomfortable to talk about. Write on, my sisters and brothers, write on!!

Thank you family, friends and those I met in passing for being an intricate part of my journey. Thank you for sharing your love, life and stories with me. They have helped me to share in this capacity. Our experiences have been my greatest source of inspiration for this book!

I dedicate this book to the lives
lost and gone too soon.
I dedicate this book to my beautiful brothers
and sisters still fighting the good fight!

George.Ahmaud.Philando.Sandra.Trayvon.Alton.Alberta.Terence.Botham.Atatiana.Laquan.Eric.
Charly.Shelly.Jamar.Michelle.Jeremy.Tanisha.Tamir.Jaron.Kayla.Walter.Jordan.Dante.
Akai.Laquan.Miriam.Stephon.Mike.Joe.Sam.Freddie.Earl.John.Paul.Keith.Henry.
Richard.Anthony.Kendrick.Everett.Kwame.Raymond.Rumain.Victor.Ahmaud.
Antron.Kevin.Korey.Yusef.Kaleif.Albert.Nathson.Jerome.Huwe.George.
Andrew.Ransom.Alfred.Christopher.De'Von.Julius.Lamonte.
Gregory.Jamarion.Ryan.Brandon.Jimmy.Rekia.Shannon.
Mark.Willie.Jemel.DeAndre.Robert.Dejuan.
Wendell.Clifford.Hubert.Samuel.Patrick.
Jonathan.Danny.Delano.
Maurice.Johnathan.
Breonna

**Above are just a few of the names of the many
men and women who died before their time.**

**The one thing they all shared - deep rich skin color.
Beneath the depth of their skin,
was a valuable and worthy soul which dwelled within.**

When will they learn?
When will we truly overcome?
Sometimes the rage and woe
creeps deep within our souls.
Yet we rise!

Fear Not My Skin, Look Deep Within!

Please tell me why our skin tone
Can cause such fright and fear
Why race makes us a target
Statistics make that clear

Our skin, to some, a weapon
A gun, a club, a knife
Our skin, to some, means danger
And threatening to a life

Please tell me how our skin tones
A gift from God you know
Can make one hate and fear us
And make some stoop so low

To call us 'thugs' and 'hoodlums'
And 'criminal' on the news...
How would those words affect you
If you walked inside our shoes?

The ones who yell it the loudest
Sometimes they hold the cross
The ones who claim to save souls
And lead the weakened lost

The things they preach not practice
Will turn some souls away
From the hatred and hypocrisy
And empty words they say

They lose more souls to darkness
By pointing reckless blame
Demonizing darker skin tones
With nerve to use His name

I don't know who their God is
Or if they know this fact
Our Jesus, son of God
Has skin with shades of black

The next time that we cross paths
I hope you see what's real
Our blackness is a blessing
Our greatness, all God's will

No one is born hating another person because
of the color of his skin, or his background
or his religion. People learn to hate, and if
they can learn to hate, they can be taught
to love, for love comes more naturally
to the human heart than its opposite.
~ Nelson Mandela

Who Taught You To Hate?

We met when we were children
By chance you sat by me
In the school we learned as classmates
So happy and so free

We had some things in common
We both liked cars and trains
We loved to play together
With trucks and bikes and planes

Each day we forged a friendship
And cherished it with pride
No care, concern or worries
About our differences outside

I saw you as my brother
You were my trusted friend
We talked without restrictions
As if we were close kin

Then one day as we walked home
We saw a dreadful sight
Two men enlocked with clenched fists
In a heated horrid fight

The men we saw, no strangers
Their faces we knew all too well
Both "leaders" in our household
Our fathers raising hell

The anger we saw inside them
So vivid and so clear
The hatred that their words spoke
Gripped us both with fear

What made them loathe each other
And draw the line that day?
What happened to the scriptures
We heard our preacher say?

'Love your neighbor as yourself
And work through all the rest
Treat each other with respect
At least try doing your best

But now my Dad hates your Dad
I'm told to hate you too
Because he says we're 'different'
Though the bond we have is true

I know God made us special
Unique in our own way
But don't we all serve one God
To whom we love and pray

Dad says we should stay separate
And that we're worlds apart
Skin color seems to judge all
And not a person's heart

So now I'm told to walk by
Each time I see your face
And find a friend just like me
Or at least in my same race.

I miss the days of freedom
When I could choose my friends
And I could live by God's word
Not by the thoughts of men

I thought that as we grew up
The wiser we would become
But the way some choose to fight
I'm sad to say seems dumb

Forgive me for my harsh words
Dear father, whom I love
But I choose not to stoop low
I'd rather rise above!

I won't pass down this evil
Or ways we separate
Instead, I'll choose to love all
And reject man's way to hate

For the child who yearned for
the love and acceptance
of his/her earthly father,
remember your heavenly Father,
your ultimate Creator,
adores you yet and still and
always, always will!
You are valuable and have always been,
regardless of who is able to recognize it.
The love missed by man is always
supplied by our Creator.
Keep rising in your worthiness!

Dear Pop

Of all the love I craved
My dad's was at the top
Affirmation and Acceptance
From the one who I called "Pop"

I never met a soul
Who didn't have that need
To know that love would pass
From father to his seed

A father gives us life
But a Daddy gives us love
Broad shoulders to support
A man who stands above

With tender loving care
Fulfilling all our needs
Consistent loving Pop
Who guides, protects and leads

But when those needs aren't met
And holes form in the heart
And fill with bitterness
From dreams all torn apart

The thoughts of plans we made
At least inside my head
Of you and me together
Just us, is what you said

My eyes fixed on the door
While waiting for the one
Who gave me life on earth
And says I am his son

Those days then turned to nights
And nights another day
Another promise lost
Did God not hear me pray?

I prayed for Pop to come
I longed for Dad to care
To show I mattered some
A soul he'd want to spare

Neck deep in my tears of grief
While trying to stay afloat
Inhaling all that pain
Yet trying not to choke

A heart that beats too fast
And veins that bleed too blue
From days of craving warmth
And hugs that came too few

I had to learn one thing
I'm going to share with you
The love of Christ is pure
It's constant, whole and true

We can't control the love
That some choose not to give
We can control our thoughts
And how we choose to live

We can forgive and heal
The wounds of brokenness
In time, God will restore
We're worthy and we're blessed!

For the child whose innocence was stripped
in ways no one should endure...
God knows your pain.
He is your Healer.

For the one who feels the hurt
Of a heart that just won't mend...
God can heal all brokenness.
And make you whole again.

For anyone who dealt with physical, sexual,
verbal and emotional abuse –
Christ is our redeemer!
You can heal and rise again!

Still I Heal

The act against your soul
By the predator, fool and thief
No longer should you suffer
And fill the holes with grief

The sin that was committed
Was never yours to bear
So rid yourself of blame
It just ain't yours to share

It's okay for you to grieve
And even wonder why
But rid yourself of guilt
Reject the devil's lie!

And don't you doubt yourself
Or who you were meant to be
Someone with strength and purpose
And a heart and mind that's free

Don't let their violation
Steal all your joy and peace
You're worthy of a healing
It's time for pain to cease

It's time to celebrate
Just who you are in Christ
It's time to rise up strong
And embrace a joyous life

Abuse is an act against the will of God.
The sin is not for the victim to bear.

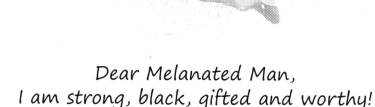

Dear Melanated Man,
I am strong, black, gifted and worthy!

As independent as I am,
I still need your protection.
I will always respect your strength
and appreciate our unity.
Remember who we are and
where we came from!
We were not created to destroy one another!

Sincerely, Melanated Women

Sincerely, Melanated Queens

Dear Melanated Man,
The one I call my friend
Who do you see
When you look deep within?

Deep in my eyes
And into my soul,
Do you see someone
You really care to know?

Dear Black Man,
My brothers, my bold and blessed kin
What do you see
Beneath my rich brown skin?

Do you see raw beauty,
And the sacred soul of a queen?
Do you see a mighty spirit,
Created by our King?

Sometimes I do though wonder
As I lay awake at night
If you can hear my gentle roar
Or recognize my light.

Do you dare cover me
As I have covered you?
Or have you turned your back
On bonds that once held true?

Am I your precious comrade
Or am I now your prey?
Do you stand beside me
To fight another day?

To fight for all our freedoms
And fight for all our lives
Pray for peaceful rest
And in the morning rise

Do you always remember
The way we overcame
And all of our brave people
Who gave so we might gain?

Enduring the whims of the wicked
With shackled hands and feet
Pouring out blood, sweat and tears
So wounds would not repeat

Our fathers took those beatings
For you and other sons
They paid a heavy price
From trees some even hung

With little but their passion
And the grace from up above
Did they survive the torture
And still find will to love

So tell me my dear brothers
And others like my kin
What do you see inside me
When you dare to look within?

Sometimes I sit and wonder
How it came to be
That some see only objects
And not a soul set free

For those who steal the spirit
Of those sold into shame

Who trade our lives for profit
In the human traffic game

Dear Melanated Man
What do you see in me?
I hope you see the people
Who fought to set us free

I hope you see a person
A heart, a mind, and a soul
I pray you see my value
And my right to grow

We have our dreams and purpose
A life of priceless worth
We are a gift from God
And have been since our birth

Dear Black Man, my brothers
And ones I need to trust
May love rule over hate
And protection over lust!

Please lift up all our daughters
And teach our sons to pray
For courage and divine strength
To rise high another day

Know it's not cool or ever God's plan
To embrace self-destruction and sin
To self-abuse or self-medicate
And follow the wreckage of men
To poison our souls with things that bring out
The wrong kind of courage and game
And make us do things that we will regret
Then live with the guilt and the shame

Escape.From.Sunken.Places.

My ride or die, my bff
The giver of that thrill
The one who stole my broken heart
And came back for my will

I should have known how strong you were
How much you could devour
The way you'd slip right through my cracks
Seduce me every hour

I thought I could just dip and dab
And use you as a crutch
Just here and there, not everywhere
But then you proved too much

So over time I tried to leave
And kick you to the curb
And play you like a jilted love
A fling that went absurd

But every time I put you down
And tried to walk away
You lured me back, for one more snack,
I was your constant prey

Hooked up to chains and shackled minds
Embraced a life of sin
Got all caught up in Satan's plan
To steal the strongest men

And make us weak and turn from God
And all that makes us strong
Confuse our minds and rot our souls
All while we're doing wrong

I smoked, I shot, and snorted too
The poison that I bought
Whatever way, I could escape
My dark, deep twisted thoughts

I lied, I stole, did what I could
To get another high
Another rush, another day
Another tearful lie

The tears I cried, the ones I've caused
A river could it fill
The hurt, the pain, betrayal too
What spirits did I kill?

So much is gone, too much was lost
The times they needed me
I have to rise and give my life
To Him who sets me free

I cried and prayed and fought so hard
To rise up above the flames
And give my life back to my Lord
And leave those deadly games

We've parted ways a million times
But know this day's the one
I say goodbye, at last to you
True living has begun

The son of God,
the man with brown skin and woolly hair,
His name is Jesus.
These truths are documented
in the Holy Bible.
It matters not what image people
choose to affix to their walls;
it doesn't change who He is.
Does the truest image, however,
change the attitude of some?
Sisters and brothers,
of all backgrounds and colors,
could you still rise
like the sun in the skies
and truly love everyone?

What would they do if they really knew?

What Would They Do If *They* Really Knew?

How would they pray and what would they say,
If the Jesus they knew looked like me?

With skin melanated, and hair thick and curly,
What would they do?

Dark caramel skin, eyes like my kin
How would they feel, how would they deal?
What would they do?

To the son of our King, would they still sing
The hymns and the songs, about rights and the wrongs?
What would they do?

The man on the cross, my Savior and Boss,
Would they still feel free, to purely love thee?
What would they do?

Would the love still be pure, and made to endure,
For the one who has died for our sins?
Would they all embrace, with all the same grace
The man who reflects all my kins?

That pic on the wall, in their bedroom or hall,
Would they still keep?
And smile every day, in the same Christian way
To the shepherd and all of His sheep.

Can they see what is sin, and one day begin
To love one another, regardless of color?

How would they feel, to know the real deal?
What would they do?

On the days we feel like we're surrounded
by darkness, pain and turmoil
and like there's only one way out
The fact that we feel means we have a soul,
a conscience and a light inside of us
that is worthy of shining
Another day, another breath, another chance
to break free.
Don't give up!
Our hearts will heal again!

Yet I Rise

Some days are long and dark, the pain intense and deep
The valleys seem too low, and mountains all too steep

It's hard for me to breathe, and fill my lungs with air
Some days it's just too much, almost too much to bear

Some thoughts that fill my head, will make a strong man weak
Fighting to think straight and find the will to speak

The voices say I'm hated, and have no real loves at all
No one to save my soul, or catch me when I fall

At times I've fallen short of what God wants from me
Or failed to be the one who others need to see

But no one feels it more, than the one whose face appears
Against the darkened light, reflected on blurred mirrors

A child who was disgraced, and left alone to fend
A broken tortured soul, and heart that just won't mend

It's hard to understand, and know the reasons why
Each day that I awake, another night I die

But yet I still hang on, His grace is why I'm here
Another day to rise, and cast away my fear

God hasn't left me yet, His love is here to stay
Just knowing that as truth, is worth another day

God created ALL of our tears
for the purpose of releasing
our pain and sorrow,
cleansing our soul and rejoicing.
It's a way in which we can express
our innermost feelings.
It is a reminder of both our human
vulnerability and great strength.
It shows heart, soul and the
ability to purge and heal.

He Wept

Real men don't cry 'cuz' they hold it inside
Deep down and hidden, all part of their pride

I say that's a folly, a myth and LIE
Real men express hurt, they weep and they cry

Real people all bleed as we deal with life's woes
It's part of our journey and how this thing goes

It's human to weep as it is to feel pain
It's natural to feel, no need to explain

So when life gets heavy and you want to release
Allow yourself freedom, to find your own peace

Through purging and weeping and cleansing the soul
Can we heal the hurt as we just let the tears roll

There's no shame in showing what's deep in your heart
So hold your head high, releasing is smart!

It sure ain't a weakness but a sign that you care
So delight in expressions and all that you share

After storms come the rainbows, and the sun after rain
With healing comes strength, rise and conquer again!

Jesus Wept. (John 11:35 NLT)

We were exquisitely designed by our Creator.
God makes no mistakes.
He has given you the tools to create
your own destiny and leave a
legacy of life, light and love.
Our lives have significance way
beyond the perception of others.
In our authenticity, we are Worthy!
Always Remember Your Worth!

True to You

At every twist and turn, the idols do we see
In magazines and books, internet and tv

They seem to have it all, yes all the man made perks
Followers, fame and fortune, material things - the works

Impressive it may seem, to live a life so large
To have an entourage, and be the one in charge

But should we base our worth on likes we get from fans
Or measure our success on tags we can command?

Should we strive to follow, and be like someone else
Or learn to grow our gifts, and learn to love thyself?

At times it gets confusing and hard to get it clear
What way to reach our goals, and how to persevere

God says to follow Him and let His spirit lead
Away from shallow thoughts, and selfishness and greed

He gave us all free will, a mind to think things through
So we can search our hearts, and to thine self be true

Let's use what God gave us, and shine in our own light
Authentic, rare, divine, amazing in His sight

No need to duplicate or imitate another
Each day you search inside, self worth you shall discover!

For anyone who felt rejected by peers
and cast aside by many,
your worth was never determined
by the opinions of others.
Rather than looking for acceptance
in the wrong places,
spend that time and energy on becoming
the best version of You!

Just The Way I Am

They called you queer and weird
And had so much to say
You told them you were fine
That God made you this way

They laughed and joked and prodded
And others joined along
Each day they kept it going
Saying that you're all wrong

Not one stood up to help
Or make the teasing stop
I guess it goes to show
How bullies stay on top

But don't they know the pain
And suffering that it brings
To beat with hurtful words
And kill the bird that sings

Let's say to all those bullies
Who thought that they were cute
The kicks you gave to others
One day you'll feel that boot

You'd better start to watch
The careless words you say
The things you do to others
Will ricochet one day

Meanwhile, for all you kids
Who take it all in stride
You are the bigger persons
So stand up tall with pride

For those of you - brave ones
Who stick up for that mate -
Kudos to you for taking
A stand against the hate

We should accept each other
And all that makes us free
And express ourselves with courage
And be who we shall be

"As I reflect back on my life, just what do I see? Who is the man staring back at me? Is it the one, I tried to become? Just who is this man in which I am one?"

Reflections, Reflections, Reflections
by J.W. Davis

Gaze into my eyes
What do you see?
Look harder, do you still recognize me?
Reflections into your own eyes...
Soul penetrated, heart rate elevated
In shrouds, masqueraded to cover up
What God created
And a life that's debated
Can you see clearly now?
Or accept what can no longer be tolerated…
In any case... hate it.

I see a king

Go ahead and say it
Cause life is a game of thrones
Go ahead and play it
There's no rewind, no holding time
And no way to delay it
Just hold your own and seek your throne
Even a mother of dragons can say it...
There's a time to keep the dragon
And another time to slay it
Know who you are and always seek truth...
Let father time, okay it!
A bright mosaic shines in the light.
Let shadows run and hide in the night
Afraid now to stand and fight
For the time has come.
The time is now and twice a day is right
Even a clock that doesn't run is showing it can be done.
So imagine running the race
It's not just to win but to begin

To run it for the rising…
and exhaling all that has been within
For happiness and dreams
Cause even mountain peaks have a base
We've all started somewhere...over and over again
At least you ran, at least you climbed
Now life you can embrace!!

The poem **WORTHY**
is dedicated to my amazing
sisters and brothers
of all races, creeds and backgrounds
who were undervalued by someone incapable
of recognizing and celebrating
their true value.

Worthy

The love you gave to them
Was never done in vain
Sometimes the ones we love
Just can't love us the same

It's not that you were bad
Or lacking in some way
It takes each one to work
It takes each one to stay

As seasons come and go
Sometimes our loves will too
The greatest love of all
So awesome and so true

It comes from up above
From the one who makes us whole
The one who gives us hope
And heals a broken soul

God knows just what you need
And the love that will complete
Just wait on Him my friend
Your partner you will meet

The one who sees your WORTH
And stands right by your side
The lasting love you want
A love that will abide

So don't you fret my friend
Or let it change your way
Stay tender and be strong
There is a brighter day

Rejection is often just redirection
to something greater coming your way.
Trust the Holy Spirit inside of You!

We are not defined by the quantity
of successes or failures
but rather the quality of love and light
we get to share with others through our
Dreams, Detours and Destinations.

Dreams.Detours.Destinations.

You thought you had the blue prints
And thought you knew the way
The goals that you had set
And would fulfill one day

But through the twists and turns
Detours your life would take
You ended up in places
With plans you didn't make

At first you were disheartened
No, 'angry', is the word
Asking 'why it didn't happen?'
The dreams you all concurred

You never planned to be
But what you had dreamed of
Giving all you had
Doing the things you love

So how did you get here
This unfamiliar space?
Not living how you desired
Or in your rightful place

You thought you'd live your dream out
Not trapped in what you dread
Searching, scrapping, hustling
To barely get ahead

You put forth all that effort
And fought for what was real
You prayed for all you wanted
The goals you would fulfill

But maybe what you prayed for
Was not the way to go
Maybe God knew better
The things you didn't know

Did you heed and listen
Before the well ran dry?
God had a different calling
And here's the reason why

As long we look outward
To make us whole within
We'll never reach our purpose
And rise above our sin

It's not about our glory
It's not about our praise
It 's all about God's kingdom
And how we fill our days

Do you support your brothers
And lift your sisters up
Protect the babes and children
Or fill the elders cup?

Do you rise each day
To spread His light and love
Not for fame and fortune
But blessings from above?

When we embrace our journey
And who we are in Christ
It's then we find our purpose
In this thing called life

To the ones who feel both
hated and imitated,
revered yet feared,
both celebrated and crucified,
the fact that in spite of it all
you still keep climbing
is a testament to your extraordinary resilience
and ability to overcome.
No matter the contradictions,
persecution and lies,
you, God's child, can rise.

#TeamKap

Revered Yet Feared

They love to see you run
And jump and catch the ball.
They love to watch you tackle
And see opponents fall.

They love to watch your strength
And marvel at your skills.
It gives the braggers rights
And gives the humble chills.

It's fun when *they* make money
And profit off your gifts.
But when you take a knee,
It's then that you have those rifts.

How dare you stand for justice!
How dare you raise up tall,
Demanding life and fairness
And freedom for us all!

How dare you bring attention
To what has always been!
How dare you call for action
To stop the deadly sin!

You've called the racists 'racist',
For that you'll pay a price.
It takes a man of courage
To make that sacrifice.

Just know real ones adore you.
A hero in our eyes,
A man of truth and honor
And one without disguise.

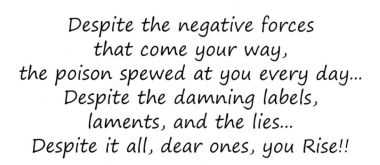

Despite the negative forces
that come your way,
the poison spewed at you every day...
Despite the damning labels,
laments, and the lies...
Despite it all, dear ones, you Rise!!

The Thin Line

They love to see you sing
And dance the night away.
They wish they had your rhythm
To move the way you sway.

The soul that you were born with
Is deep within your core.
The thing that makes you special
The thing real friends adore.

But sometimes that adoration
Can turn the color green.
The thing they love about you
Can also make them mean.

The very thing they worship
And copy when they can
Can be a source of envy
For the jealous turning man.

Dear one, now you be careful
And watch who you let near.
Some will love to hate you
When shine induces fear.

For Malcolm, Mike and Nipsey
They learned that lesson late.
That some will hold you high
Then lure you into fate.

You can't control what's in them,
The loathing of themselves.
One day we pray they realize
The salt goes on the shelves.

To love each one, no different
This one, that one and me.
Those isms kill our nature,
But acceptance sets us free.

I AM BLACK ENOUGH!

Black Enough was written by Connor G. Mason at the age of 16 – a very pivotal time in his life – a time he felt the sting of the all mighty isms. Like the air we breathe, like the sun in the skies, my dear child, We Rise!

Black Enough
Written by Connor G. Mason

Am I black enough, do I have the right talk...or the right walk?
Is my complexion not dark enough like others...
the ones who I'm supposed to call my brothers?
Is it because I value my education or my strong
resistance to peer temptation?
Am I black enough?
Why must I speak slang at all times
knowing there are other words to express how I feel?
Why can't I choose my own way to say what I believe to be real?
Should my pants sag so low I look like a clown?
Not the look I'm going for…
Rather be a king with a crown.
You dare to tell me what shoes I should wear?
Unless you are paying, why do you care?
Why can't I expand my music to more than just rap?
Some of it fills our minds with meaningless crap!
Am I black enough?
No race has disowned me more than my own.
After all we've been through, you'd think we'd have grown.
All of my brothers, listen to my plea
as long as we hate each other, we'll never be free.
Don't let all of our progress become ancient.
Together we can make this place a better nation.

If we want to rise as a people,
we must get rid of
destructive stereotypes, labels and isms.
They only serve to divide and conquer us.
We are truly so much better and
worthy of so much more!

Let's take steps to sincerely love our
brothers and sisters regardless of skin tone,
dialect, fashion preference, hair texture,
economic status or anything external.
Let's choose to give each other the support
and respect we are worthy of.
In the sight of our Creator, we are all worthy!

If we want others to respect the diversity
within our race/culture, we must first lead the
way. We must lead by example by respecting
ourselves and those within our own families,
communities, cultures, countries and planet.

Shame and secrecy will keep us in bondage
but the Truth shall set us free!
God's light will give us life.
Choose light over darkness

From Darkness to Light

I never understood how it's not good
To follow the lead of what's right
For speaking up front, not taking the brunt,
And bringing awareness to the light.

Why must we hide and then let them slide,
And not face what we know to be true?
How will you feel if you had to deal
With taking your turn as the fool?

The brave one who speaks, some call them 'leaks,'
Are shamed for what they might say.
For calling out wrong and singing that song,
For making all predators pay.

It's time that we stand, upfront like a man
And do all we know to be right.
Lift up one another, and pray for our brother
And challenge what's wrong in God's sight.

Things like hair wither and shed,
but the love we have for ourselves and
others can grow and last for a lifetime.
What matters most is what's growing within.

Crown & Glory Within

When we need some support,
Someone to lift us up,
It's your love we need, my friend,
To help fill our empty cup.

We look not for a strand,
That's no more than a thread
Our souls are not defined
By what sits on our head.

We look for something greater,
A voice to say 'I care.'
And arms to hug and hold
And not for locks of hair.

So what lies deep in us
Is much more than a thing.
It's patience, care and love
That makes a sad heart sing.

So please don't place your worth
On things that don't give life
Or wash away our cares
Or help us deal with strife.

It was never the outer things
That made them love you so.
It was your warmth and grace
And that amazing glow.
Things like hair and nails
May decorate the shell,
But the love we give to others
Is what really makes us well.

God created you wonderfully,
uniquely and beautifully...
so be YOU!
You are authentically Be You Tiful!
Stand in your power,
walk in your purpose
and rest with God's peace!

Remember who you are
and what you're made of!

Luvin' My Authenticity

Love it thick, love it thin, all the coils in your hair.
Love the locks and the waves and the braids that you wear.

Love the skin you're in that covers you like fine silk.
Deep chocolate, golden bronze, honey, caramel, mocha milk

Love you big, love you lean, love you short, love you tall.
Love your features, each unique, love each one, flaws and all!

Love your twang and your drawl and the loving way you speak.
Love the way that you express and the knowledge that you seek.

Love the depth in your soul that makes a sad heart sing.
Masterpiece, one of a kind, created by the King of kings.

Explore within, develop your skills, live a life that serves you well.
Pursue your dreams, build your teams,
work, learn, love, rise, and excel!!

Know Thy Worth!!

This poem was inspired by all of my incredibly strong, gifted, brave and brilliant brothers and sisters who never cease to amaze me.

Magnificent Melanation

Our people are from the parts
Where the sun just loves to shine
And the land is rich with treasures,
Some exotic and one of a kind.

The place they call our motherland
A place where our ancestors grew,
A place we once walked with freedom
And the place where our native flag flew.

Red, black and green
Are the colors that tell our story.
Red for our blood and green for our land
And black for our grace and our glory.

Remember the past and stay woke in the present.
Forget not from where you descend,
The queens and the kings and heirs to the throne,
You come from great royalty kin

They gave you the great depth, undeniable strength
And the richness of your melanated skin,
The mind to rise high and the heart to go deep
Are the treasures you will carry within.

No bondage, no limits, no prison, no walls
Free in mind, body, spirit and soul
Believe in yourself and live in your purpose
Remember the truth that you know

Stand tall, shoulders back, be humble and proud
As you walk with your head held up high
Speak up for yourself and fight for your rights
Look the enemy right straight in the eye.

Fear not the ones who try to oppress
And make you feel less than a man
You were made in His image, blessed with great gifts
To rise from the ashes and sand.

This land is my temporary home

When It's Time, Reach for me Father
I won't be afraid

What's It Like, My Father?

What's it like my father,
In your final resting place?
What's it like my father,
Are you glad you left this race?

What's it like my father,
Do you see me from where you are?
What's it like my father,
I see you in every star.

What's it like my father,
Do you ever miss it here?
What's it like my father,
To live without pain, shame or fear?

What's it like my father,
To be in our Lord's warm embrace?
What's it like my father,
To meet Jesus face to face?

What's it like my father,
To be home so safe and sound?
What's it like my father,
To have risen from this battleground?

What's it like my father?
Will you reach for me one day?
What's it like my father,
Will you help me find my way?

Reflections

Over the years, I've often reflected back on what has sustained me during my darkest hours and lowest points. It wasn't the money I had in the bank or my physical reflection in the mirror. It wasn't the things I had achieved or the degrees I had earned. It wasn't any privilege I may have had or any opportunities afforded to me. It wasn't even the roof over my head, the food at my disposal or the ones who I called friends. While valuable indeed, those weren't the things that ultimately kept me from going under during the highest tides and lowest valleys. It was my belief in my Creator. It was my belief in my worth, a higher purpose for my existence and my determination to rise from any ashes and find peace, through it all. I had to replace any negative messages swirling in my head with self-affirming messages like 'I am an extraordinary being created in the image of God, exquisitely designed, African in decent, varied by birth, born to live in my power, walk in my purpose and rest in God's peace…not to be compared to or defined by any man but by the grace given to me from the day of my birth. Struggles and hardships are a real part of life that cannot define, defeat nor deplete me. Glory to God and our Lord and Savior who keeps keeping us!

Acknowledgements

To my amazing family, Thank you, thank you, thank you for standing by me, believing in me, covering me and loving me - through it all. I am deeply grateful for all of your support and inspiration. We're in this together, until the end! I 'agape' love you!

To all the men and women, family by blood and/or friendship, our experiences keep me both grounded and rising higher. Love, power, grace & peace to you all!

To All Of My Brothers and Sisters, of every color and creed,
Rise in LOVE, PEACE, & POWER
Stay forever WISE, WOKE, & WORTHY

Dear Ones, Like the Sun In The Skies,
Let Us Rise!

Printed in the United States
by Baker & Taylor Publisher Services